by William Anthony

BEARPORT
PUBLISHING

Minneapolis, Minnesota

**Bearport Publishing Company Product Development Team**
President: Jen Jenson; Director of Product Development: Spencer Brinker; Managing Editor: Allison Juda; Associate Editor: Naomi Reich; Associate Editor: Tiana Tran; Senior Designer: Colin O'Dea; Associate Designer: Elena Klinkner; Associate Designer: Kayla Eggert; Product Development Specialist: Anita Stasson

*Library of Congress Cataloging-in-Publication Data*

Names: Anthony, William (Children's author), author.
Title: Disgusting diseases / by William Anthony.
Description: Minneapolis, Minnesota : Bearport Publishing Company, [2024] | Series: Hideous history | Includes bibliographical references and index.
Identifiers: LCCN 2023010553 (print) | LCCtN 2023010554 (ebook) | ISBN 9798888220269 (library binding) | ISBN 9798888222164 (paperback) | ISBN 9798888223413 (ebook)
Subjects: LCSH: Communicable diseases--History--Juvenile literature. | Diseases and history--Juvenile literature.
Classification: LCC RC113 .A58 2024 (print) | LCC RC113 (ebook) | DDC 616.9--dc23/eng/20230308
LC record available at https://lccn.loc.gov/2023010553
LC ebook record available at https://lccn.loc.gov/2023010554

For more information, write to Bearport Publishing, 5357 Penn Avenue South, Minneapolis, MN 55419

# CONTENTS

# PIECES OF THE PAST

Secrets are everywhere. You just have to know where to look. Weapons, tools, bodies, and even buildings may be buried below your feet.

The past was not easy for those living through it.

Crime and disaster were everywhere. War was always just around the corner. And if those things didn't get you, mysterious illnesses might.

It's time to take a journey into the past. Are you ready to learn about the hideous history of gory diseases? It's not for the faint-hearted.

# RAT PROBLEMS

In medieval times, cities were much dirtier than they are today. People smelled really bad because they didn't bathe. Rodents and insects spread diseases, including the bubonic **plague**.

The bubonic plague was disgusting. People sick with it grew big bumps on their skin called buboes. These spots were black and painful. Sometimes, they burst!

There were not many hospitals or doctors around back then. So, the plague was very deadly.

One wave of bubonic plague started in China around 1334. The disease spread from there. Some **historians** think it killed up to 60 percent of the people living in Europe at the time!

# PEOPLE AND POX

Smallpox was one of the deadliest diseases in the world. Yet, the story of smallpox is not just about how horrible and scary it was. It has a human victory, too!

Smallpox gave people red spots and **sores** all over their skin. Some people were able to live through their sickness. But many died.

Things started to change in 1796. A man named Edward Jenner heard some people were getting a less-deadly disease called cowpox. They did not catch smallpox after that.

Jenner tested this by giving a young boy cowpox. The boy never caught smallpox. Using this idea, scientists created **vaccines** that were able to stop people from getting smallpox!

# NO ONE IS SAFE

Leprosy is a horrible disease. It can make people lose feeling in parts of their body. Their skin can become bumpy. Some people even go blind.

At one time, leprosy could make anyone sick. It could strike the common people or even royalty.

Jerusalem's King Baldwin IV had leprosy from a young age. Because of the sickness, he couldn't feel anything in his right arm.

The disease got worse as he got older. However, Baldwin IV still fought on the battlefield to protect Jerusalem. He won big battles against other armies while also fighting his leprosy!

# WHO KNOWS?

A terrible disease struck Athens, Greece, between 430 and 427 BCE. About 100,000 people died. But even today, we're not sure what they died from.

There is not much information about the disease. This is why historians can't tell us what happened.

Only one man made any record about the sickness. His name was Thucydides, and he caught the disease himself. He wrote that he had red eyes, patches of skin filled with pus, and blood in his mouth.

At the time, Greece was at war. The people of Athens were trying to defend their land. But the disease wiped out many of their soldiers.

Being sick today is not the same as it was a long time ago. Today, typhoid would give you a headache, a cough, and a fever.

TYPHOID MARY

If you got typhoid long ago, you would probably have died! However, you might not have known you were sick right away. This happened to one woman who came to be nicknamed Typhoid Mary.

More than 100 years ago, she infected many people without knowing it. A doctor tried to check Mary, but she chased him away with a carving fork!

Mary was eventually taken to a cottage away from everyone. She was put in **quarantine**. This stopped the deadly disease from spreading any further.

# ARRRRRGH, THAT'S NOT GOOD

Pirates are scary. Pirates with horrible teeth and bad breath are scarier. Between the 1400s and 1700s, this might be exactly the type of pirate you would meet.

Many pirates had a disease called scurvy. They got scurvy because they didn't eat enough foods that had vitamin C.

ORANGES AND LEMONS BOTH HAVE VITAMIN C.

Pirates with scurvy often had bleeding gums. The skin on their gums would turn black.

Their only chance to get better came from getting some vitamin C. However, it was very hard to find fresh food out at sea!

# DAILY POISON

Throughout history, people have turned to lead as a cheap and useful metal.

LEAD COINS

It was used in makeup, coins, and the dishes people ate from. There was one problem with lead, though. It is very, very poisonous.

QUEEN ELIZABETH I WORE MAKEUP MADE WITH LEAD.

When lead got into people's bodies, it caused lead poisoning. This gave them pain in their muscles, stomachs, or heads. It also made them look wrinkly and old.

In really bad cases, it would even affect people's minds. Unfortunately, people used lead for absolutely everything. As you can probably guess, it didn't end well for many. . . .

# TOO MUCH BLOOD

Have you ever gone to the doctor when you're sick? What have they done for you?

If you went to an ancient Roman or Greek doctor, you might have gotten a different **treatment**. The doctor might have thought you had too much blood in your body. Then, they might offer to let some out.

This was called bloodletting. In the past, bloodletting was used to **cure** all sorts of things. A doctor might even cut you open for a headache!

The idea that a person had too much blood was often wrong. In fact, losing blood in this way caused some people to die.

# THE LAST DANCE

One day in 1518, a woman in Strasbourg, in what is now France, started dancing. There was no music or reason for Frau Troffea to dance. But she did.

At first, people laughed and cheered her on. However, Frau Troffea didn't stop. She continued dancing day after day. Soon, others joined her.

By the sixth day, 34 people were dancing. They were all struck with a very strange disease. People danced until they were too tired or died from heart attacks.

Some historians think the dancing disease was caused by eating something bad. To this day, no one knows exactly what happened.

# IT WAS ALL YELLOW

Yellow fever was a horrible disease. People would get **aches** in their bodies and would throw up. For some, things would only get worse from there.

These people might start to turn yellow. They might even start to bleed from their mouths, noses, and eyes. Then, they would die.

For years, most doctors thought the disease was spread from person to person. They were very wrong.

The cause of the disease came from tiny insects. Mosquitoes carried it and passed it on when they bit people.

**MOSQUITO**

# THE DISEASE OF MANY NAMES

Tuberculosis has been killing people for thousands of years. Now, most people just call it TB. However, it hasn't always had that name.

In ancient Greece, Hippocrates wrote about a sickness. He called it phthisis. But it was TB all along.

There was a disease during the Middle Ages that people called the King's Evil. It was really TB, too. People thought they would get better from the sickness if the king touched them. They didn't.

TB was often called consumption during the 19th century.

# A HOLE IN THE HEAD

How far back in history do you think surgery goes? One type dates back at least 6,000 years. It was called trephination.

This was a pretty brutal surgery. People would use a special tool to drill a hole into someone's skull.

Many **experts** think this might have been a way of treating head injuries or of getting rid of pain. Others think it might have been done to treat diseases of the mind.

But this treatment has not stayed in the past. Doctors still drill holes into the skull to treat some head injuries today!

It's okay, you can stop covering your eyes now. Let your breathing slow down. The past was a gruesome place to be, but you are not living there now.

Lots of people in the past met frightening ends. Their horrible stories showed no one was safe from disease!

# GLOSSARY

**aches** pains throughout the body

**cure** to get rid of an illness completely

**experts** people who have special skills or knowledge about a particular subject

**historians** people who study what happened in the past

**plague** a disease that spread quickly and killed many people

**quarantine** to keep away from other people to stop the spread of an illness

**sores** painful spots on the body

**treatment** medical fixes for illnesses or pain

**vaccines** things that are given to people to protect them from getting sick from a specific disease

# INDEX

# READ MORE

**Gunasekara, Mignonne.** *Death by Blundering Bodies (Disastrous Deaths)*. Minneapolis: Bearport Publishing, 2022.

**Havemeyer, Janie.** *Smallpox: How a Pox Changed History (Infected!)*. North Mankato, MN: Capstone Press, 2019.

**Torres, John A.** *Petrifying Plagues (Creepy, Kooky Science)*. New York: Enslow Publishing, 2020.

# LEARN MORE ONLINE

1. Go to **www.factsurfer.com** or scan the QR code below.

2. Enter "**Disgusting Disease**" into the search box.

3. Click on the cover of this book to see a list of websites.